MW01258116

How To Rescue Your Marriage

Proven Advice To Help Overcome Conflicts And Save Your Marriage Forever

Alexis G. Roldan

www.RoldanBooks.com/AlexisOptin

Table of Contents

Introduction 3

Chapter 1: Why There Are Conflicts In Marriage 5

Chapter 2: How You Can Overcome Conflicts 11

Chapter 3: How To Resolve Conflicts And Save Your Marriage 21

Chapter 4: Restoring Love Into Your Marriage 28

Chapter 5: Choosing A Marriage Counselor 34

Chapter 6: Turning Conflict Into Ways To Grow 38

Chapter 7: Tips For Starting A Productive Conversation 41

Conclusion 49

Introduction

I want to thank you for purchasing "How to Rescue Your Marriage".

This book contains proven steps and strategies on how you can overcome conflicts in your marriage and save it for a lifetime. You can rescue your marriage however bad you think things have gone by following the advice in this book, which has worked for many couples. This book offers solutions to marital problems and paves the way for the happy life that is intended in marriage.

There is no way to avoid conflicts in marriage. What needs to be understood is how to deal with them in order to save your marriage. This book offers you the steps and strategies you can follow to resolve any type of conflict. It solves many couples' questions about why there are conflicts in marriage, how can they resolve them, and how they can restore love and happiness in their marriage. You may feel like your marriage has hit rock bottom, but you can rescue it and find love and happiness again; it's not too late. Few couples like to admit that they have problems, but conflicts are common in all marriages. All couples have had their share of conflicts, whether they admit it or not. And for some couples, these disagreements have led to separation or divorce. It is important, therefore, to resolve conflicts as early as possible so you can save your marriage by following what is recommended in this resourceful book.

Here's a preview of what you should expect to learn from this book:

- Why conflicts even arise to begin with in every marriage
- Techniques to help you effectively overcome all conflicts
- Ways to find resolution and restore your marriage forever
- How to rekindle feelings of love that brought you together
- How to find the right type of outside help for your situation

Thank you again for purchasing this book, I hope you enjoy it!

Chapter 1: Why There Are Conflicts In Marriage

Anna and Dave have just returned from their honeymoon. They are both excited to start their life together. Just starting out, they have rented their first apartment, picked out some décor, and are set to bring it all together. On their first night home, Anna notices that Dave has left his dirty socks on the floor next to the bed. Anna is an extremely tidy person and likes order. She chooses to overlook the socks for the moment. Maybe he will pick them up in a few minutes. An hour later, she sees that they are still there. It is obvious that Dave isn't going to pick them up. With a sigh of frustration, Anna picks up the socks and puts them in the hamper. Maybe it is a one-time occurrence. The next night, the same thing happens. Anna lets the irritation build up until one night, she yells at Dave and accuses him of being a sloppy pig. Dave takes offense to this, and the couple have their first big fight: over a pair of socks! Why is this?

One of the fundamental reasons why many people have conflicts in their marriage is because of the old saying "opposites attract". You may have simply been attracted to someone with a different personality than yours. Maybe their upbringing was different from yours. In many cases, your spouse added something different to your life, bringing some sort of variety to spice up your life that you didn't have before. To overcome conflicts and save your marriage from disaster, you should always appreciate what each one of you brings into the marriage. Having someone who loves you just the way you are is a blessing. But what happens when two lovebirds start having conflicts? How do you resolve them without hurting each other? How do you save your marriage for the time being and forever? Since everyone is different, every marriage will inevitably have conflicts. To some extent, your differences complement each other and when you appreciate that, you are able to see how that happens.

Think about it: when we come together in marriage, we are pulling two different backgrounds and life experiences. One person is used to doing things one way, while the other is comfortable with the way that he or she has always done it. Even though the problem may not be apparent for some time, the differences in doing this one thing irritates the other person, causing friction in the relationship. It is important to remember that these trials are going to arise, no matter how much you know about your spouse. When you're so frustrated with your spouse, it may be time to look back to when you met and dated.

What did you admire in your spouse before you got married? After you have been married for a while these attractions, which originally brought you together, stand in the way. Some couples cannot even imagine how they got hooked to someone so different from them. We say that love is blind. After marriage is when you start noticing the attractions are differences. These differences stand out and you cannot tolerate each other. Starting a marriage with two different people, different personalities, and different expectations of each other, makes conflicts unavoidable. Add that to the daily trials of life and you will see where tensions come from. It becomes even worse when spouses lose trust. For example, it can be difficult to regain trust when an extra-marital affair is involved. The couple is bound to have conflict which cannot be avoided.

Even if you and your spouse are similar, there will still be occasions of conflict. For example, you may share the flaw of always having to be right when a disagreement comes up. Being similar in this way can lead to a long and drawn out argument. This can also lead to knowing how to get to your spouse when you're angry. Conflict can arise in any relationship, no matter how similar or different you are from your spouse. Sadly enough, many couples give up when these difficulties arise. That is why we see so many divorces happening in our society. It has become much easier to disagree and let go than to disagree and work it out.

Since every marriage has its own tensions, avoiding them is not the solution, although it can help, but it is not how you should ultimately deal with them. Conflict resolution, if handled well, can lead to a development of closeness instead of isolation. You should, therefore, discuss with your spouse how you will act when conflicts occur and how you will resolve them amicably. Conflicts can start immediately after marriage, before you say, "I do", or after you have settled down. You may start arguing over small matters that irritate you and place blame on your spouse. Your spouse might reiterate by blaming you. Before you know it, things are out of control. The accusations and counter-accusations cause hurt feelings. Having a way to look at your conflicts and agreeing on it can help avoid unnecessary pain.

If you don't resolve these problems in the right way, conflicts can become the norm. You soon find that your backgrounds and personalities are so different that you wonder how you came together in the first place, and what attracted you to each other to reach a point of getting married. Sadly enough, people shut down in the face of conflict. There are people who hope that if the problem is ignored, then it will eventually go away on its own. This can lead to resentment and hurt when the problem won't "fix itself." It's important to face and resolve your conflicts rationally in order to move forward.

At this point, it is important to understand the differences between you and your spouse, and try as much as possible to accept and adjust to them. At times you may think it's impossible, but remember where there is a will, there is a way. Your spouse is a gift that completes you in many ways, which you may not have uncovered yet. You may have come from two different countries, cultures, and backgrounds, so you will have different characters, beliefs, habits, and values. Think about it this way, even if you were siblings you would still have differences. Some of these differences can become apparent early in your marriage, though, so you need to work them out before they ruin your marriage.

Anger management
Explosive anger hurts your relationships with your spouse, kids, family, and friends. It causes lasting scars in the people you love most and it can get in the way of resolving conflicts. You need to manage your anger and fight fairly if you want to end up with a win-win scenario, especially

7

if you or your spouse is hot-tempered. It is also important to understand that anger can be expressed in many different ways. Some handle it with violence, while some may say hurtful words or yell. No matter how the anger may be expressed, it still has the potential to harm your spouse.

Anger is a natural emotion we all experience, but you should not let it control you. It is all right to become upset at someone when they do something wrong, but your relationship will break down if you don't "fight fair". A spouse who cannot hold their temper can plague a marriage, especially when the anger gets out of control. Before things can be rectified, the marriage heads to the rocks. When you fight fair, you express yourself positively and you respect the other people involved, whether it's your spouse, kids, family, neighbors, or friends.

Here are some things you can do

Make your marriage your top priority: Maintain and strengthen your marriage by making it your top priority rather than trying to win the argument. Respect the other person and their viewpoint. Come to mutual agreements and talk everything through. This is the person that you have vowed to spend the rest of your life with. Make this person a priority and make your relationship a priority.

Choose your battles wisely: Conflicts that arise in marriages can be very draining. Therefore, you should consider whether what you are arguing about is worth your time and energy. Pick your battles wisely and avoid arguing over petty issues. Simply walking away when the initial urge to argue arises can sometimes stop a conflict before it even begins.

Focus on the present conflict: When you are in a heated debate and arguing your point, it is easy to bring past hurts into the argument. This will not help. Focus on the present conflict and see what you can do to solve the problem. The past happened in the past and has been resolved. Don't throw your spouse's past wrongs back at them. This will only add to your conflict, making the argument worse.

Forgive: Resolving a conflict is impossible if you are not willing to forgive and move on. However much you punish the other person who has wronged you, you will not compensate your losses. It will only drain your relationship more. Some conflicts may be difficult to forgive, but learning to seek forgiveness is the first step in relieving yourself of the emotional stress that conflict can cause.

Know when to let go: Some people hold on to their side of the argument, even when they can't come to an agreement. If your argument is getting you nowhere, choose to discontinue it and move on. Also, the matter that you're arguing about may be petty and not even worth your time and the hurt an argument will cause. It is better to agree to disagree than to keep arguing for the sake of it. Furthermore, your marriage is much more important than winning an argument.

Understanding that conflict is a normal part of any relationship will help you to cope with it when it does present itself. No matter how perfect a relationship may seem, there will always be times when conflict will arise. It's how conflict is handled that determines how well a marriage progresses. Finding ways to handle conflict constructively will help your marriage to grow stronger rather than making it fall apart.

Exercise: Getting to Know You

Conflict can easily happen when two lives come together. Knowing and understanding your spouse's likes and dislikes can help you curb some of the conflicts. We all have our pet peeves. Learn what your spouse likes and dislikes so that you can help keep the peace in your household.

In this exercise, you will get to know some facts about each other that can hopefully prevent some conflicts.

- Grab two sheets of paper and pens. Give one to your spouse and take one for you.
- Have your spouse write down ten things that you may not know about them. You write down ten things he or she may not know about you.
- Each of you write down five to ten questions that you would like to ask the other about themselves.
- Share your little known facts with one another.
- Ask and answer the questions that you wrote down.

By the end of this exercise, you will know more about your spouse and what they like and don't like. You may not realize that your spouse has a special pet peeve that you tend to display often! Avoiding some behaviors can help to sidestep conflict in your marriage.

Getting to know your spouse and learning even more about him or her as you pursue your life together will make living together more peaceful. Conflict often results from misunderstandings. If Anna and Dave would have understood what bothered the other from the beginning, then they would have found better ways of working things out before a little problem became a huge argument.

Chapter 2: How You Can Overcome Conflicts

You may have been married for years or just a few months. For a while, things were great. You got along, you enjoyed one another, and you thought that your life together couldn't get any better. Then one day, conflict butts its ugly head into the picture. You tried to ignore it at first. After all, what is irritating you isn't necessarily a big deal. However, after some time, you find that your little problem has become a huge problem in your marriage. You cannot take it any longer. Something has to change.

Since we have established that no marriage is free from conflict, it is important that you learn how to overcome it when it presents yourself in relationship. Having a constructive resolution plan in place will help you to solve your difficulties when they come about with little difficulty. Conflict and constructive conflict resolution can actually strengthen your marriage and your relationship.

Your marriage may seem to be in pieces right now. The conflicts outnumber the good times, and you have no idea how you are going to get past these problems. Just remember, you are taking the first step to rescuing your marriage by looking for resources. In this chapter, I will give you some suggestions on ways you can overcome conflict in your relationship.

You can overcome conflicts as a couple at your own initiative by applying the following:

Love

Marriage is based on love, and if you need to save your relationship, you need to go back to what brought you together, and treasure those early moments. You can restore that love even when you think it is impossible to do so. Think about what attracted you to your spouse. In the early days of your marriage, there was a chemistry that might seem like it's not there anymore. How did that chemistry show itself? Can you go back to the places that you felt the strongest connections at? Knowing what made you fall in love in the first place is a great first step in restoring a seemingly lost relationship.

Love is a choice. At first, you may have felt those sparks, but they don't seem to be there anymore. Does that mean you should call it quits? No. You should work on your marriage and remember you made a commitment to your spouse. When you started, you saw many wonderful qualities in your spouse. They are still there if you focus on them. Choosing to look past the problems and focus on your love and your relationship can help you to resolve conflicts much easier.

If you're at a point where communication has been cut off, try communicating in different ways. Show your spouse that you care for him or her by doing things that they appreciate. This will show that you are making an effort to cater to their likes and needs. As you show them that you're trying to please them, the lines of communication will clear up and allow you to talk through some of your marital issues.

Commitment
Conflicts are easier to solve when both people are committed to their marriage. How do you know that the commitment is there? Well, you're still together and trying to work out your problems. That takes commitment right there. If you feel like the commitment is one-sided, then it's time to figure out why the commitment isn't returned by the other party.

Can you save your marriage alone? Probably not. Usually, the two of you need to work on your marriage together, but if the other person is not willing or does not see the need, there is still a chance you can rescue it alone. Taking the steps to try and save your marriage right now will show them that you really do you're your spouse and that you care about the outcome of the relationship. Maybe later, your spouse will realize and appreciate your efforts. You might just be on different levels at the moment. So, do your part and become committed. If you already know that you're committed, show your spouse the extent of your caring. After all, you are the one reading this book, so obviously you see the need to rescue your marriage.

Praise

People like praise. In fact, we are practically brought up in a world where we seek praise and rewards for the things we do. You can win over your spouse with praise placed at appropriate times. Be genuine and praise him or her for something they do or have done. This can ease tensions, especially if you base the praise on something real and it is not just flattery. There are many positive things in each of you. Surprise your spouse by praising him or her for something he or she did and do it when they least expect it. This will show your spouse that you notice his or her efforts to make your lives better.

Praise him instead of criticizing him. You catch more flies with honey then vinegar. He may have bought you a bouquet of flowers, so appreciate that when he expects a confrontation. This will be a great surprise and will encourage new behavior. How about saying "Thank you" for the delicious dinner she prepared? This can help turn things around. If you notice your spouse is busy, try taking care of a few of her errands for her to show her that you appreciate all she does for you.

Just remember, praise needs to be genuine and not forced. If your spouse thinks that you are being insincere, then it may cause even more conflict in your marriage. Don't praise your spouse unless you really do appreciate the words or the actions that they have put forth. Otherwise, they will perceive it as a way to mock them and their efforts.

Communicate

Marriage counselors recommend open communication between spouses. There is no way to know what your spouse expects or what they want unless you communicate clearly. Express your feelings to each other, but do it calmly. When there are conflicts in any relationship, communication channels can become blocked. Others communicate negatively by throwing insults at their spouses. This is hurtful. Open communication is a key factor in finding resolutions to your marital problems.

If your lines of communication are already blocked, find constructive ways to open them up so that you can have a civil and constructive conversation that can resolve matters between you. Discussing your problems is the fastest way to find a way to resolve them. However, it needs to be done in a civil way in order to avoid even more conflict.

Communication has a lot of power. If your marriage is suffering, then the best way to get through the problems is by discussing them in a civilized way. Learning constructive communication will help you to relate better to your spouse and avoid even more conflict that can result from miscommunication.

Respect

You should respect your spouse if you want respect in return. This is important because it will teach your kids to respect you as well. Always lead by example. When they see how you treat your spouse, they will treat their spouse the same way in return. It may be hard to respect someone who doesn't respect you, but take the initiative and respect your partner. Taking the time to show them that you do value their thoughts, values and opinions will help them to realize that they are a powerful part of the relationship.

A common quote is "to do unto others as you want done unto you." Practice that on a daily basis with your spouse. If you show them respect repeatedly, they will begin to see the value of respect in the relationship and reciprocate. Even if you dislike how the act or what they say, still respect them and show them that they matter as a part of the overall relationship.

Use "I" statements

"I" statements talk about you, not your partner's behavior. This will make them more likely to listen because you are not attacking them directly. For example, "You always come home late" is a statement that speaks about your partner's behavior. Such confrontations hardly change that behavior; in fact, they often just worsen the problem. Try something like, "I find it difficult to handle the children alone when you come home late." This encourages discussion and opens avenues for resolving the problem because you have talked about the problem without attacking.

Be careful, though, because some sentences that start with I are not "I" statements like saying, "I am the one who always takes the rubbish bin out." Substitute this with "I wish you would help with the trash." Avoid statements that create tension.

Think before you speak. If you know that the statement will come out harsh, try thinking of a more constructive way to state it. The last thing that you want to do is to accuse your spouse and cause conflict that way. You want your "I" statements to open up the gates of communication, not cause more tension in the relationship. Also, when using an "I" statement, try to include ways to empathize with how your spouse feels. For example, "I know that you're feeling tired, but I really could use some more help around the house," is much more constructive than, "I always do everything around the house." You are recognizing what they are feeling, but you are also stating how you feel.

Listen to your spouse

Listening is an important skill that you should practice with everyone, particularly with your spouse. Listen attentively to what your spouse is saying and seek to understand his or her point of view. Seeing a situation from his or her point of view will help you to think more rationally when a problem arises. Many arguments are a result of poor listening skills. This should be a two-sided conversation. Try asking questions to gain the clarity you need. This will help you better understand his or her viewpoint, and you will see things from their angle more clearly than if you think you know how they are feeling. Never assume.

Most people are good at talking, but poor at listening. Barriers in communication can complicate things. You may say something, but your spouse misunderstands. Try to listen so that you can understand exactly what your spouse is saying. Encourage your spouse to hear your point of view as well. If you can constructively talk and listen as a couple, many of your problems will be resolved more quickly than if you take what your spouse says and twist it to your understanding.

Take time to listen. This could be a major key in repairing a problem marriage!

Handle one issue at a time

When you are having discussions, stick to only one issue at a time. Do not bring up all of the issues at the same time because you may fail to resolve any of them. Deal with one problem and when you solve that one, only then should you move to another one.

If it helps, make a list of what you wish to discuss before sitting down and talking. This will ensure that you are addressing what you need to talk about and not forget about it. It will also help you to be able to focus on the discussion at hand without feeling like you will forget another pressing issue during your conversation.

Focus on the problem

You should focus on the problem instead of the person who caused the problem. If you have problems with finances and how your spouse spends the money, deal with the finances — not the person causing the problem. Attacks and counter-attacks only heighten the problem, making tempers flare-up. To resolve such conflicts, focus your attention on the problem only.

Before you even begin the conversation, ask yourself what the problem is and how it can be resolved. Don't point fingers at your spouse. You are in the situation together, and you are both responsible for figuring out how to deal with it. Put the problem out there and think of ways in which it can be resolved. Taking on the problems together will help your relationship grow, no matter what the problem may be.

Put limits to your listening

Listening to your spouse is a crucial part of communication, but you should put limits on listening. Giving each other time to talk and listen to what needs to be said is one of the greatest gifts you can offer your spouse, but there has to be a limit on when, where, and how. You cannot listen immediately, for example, when you are supervising your children's homework, cooking, driving, or completing other activities. There is a time for everything. When you are ready to listen, you should be free of any other distractions. This will help you to focus on the matter and not feel like your attention is needed elsewhere.

If your partner is insistent upon speaking with you, calmly tell your spouse that you will listen later, but you cannot listen right now. That way, he will know that you are not ignoring him but are willing to listen to him later.

When you do discuss a problem, make sure that you do so when you are both calm and rational. If you throw insults, the other person has a right to say, "You can't talk to me like that." You are in a relationship that demands mutual respect. There is no way for you to show respect if you are insulting them. The same thing will go for your spouse. If you feel as though he is insulting you, you have the right to tell him not to speak to you in that manner and request that you speak once he has calmed down.

Forgive

Resolving conflict requires forgiveness. There is no way around it. Couples should forgive each other because no matter how much they love and cherish each other, if they can't forgive, the relationship will always fail. No one is perfect. When someone fails, they will hurt their significant other. The only way you can deal with hurtful feelings is to forgive. Release that urge to punish or hit back. You should forgive if you expect to be forgiven in turn.

Remember, no one is perfect. We are imperfect beings trying to make our lives work with another person. This is not an easy task. Be willing to forgive and ask for forgiveness when you are the one who is wrong in the situation. This will help you to form a mutual respect for one another because you are admitting that neither of you is perfect, but you are willing to admit fault and accept forgiveness.

Focus on behavior instead of character

Pinpointing what your spouse did to you and attacking their character can emotionally assassinate him or her. Saying, "You are like this," makes your spouse defensive. Try to deal with the behavior, not the character. Explain what you expect him or her to do and offer solutions.

We all have bad habits that could be corrected. Tearing your spouse apart based on a bad habit will only make him or her more defensive when confronted. Behaviors can be changed, but attacking someone's character makes them feel like they are the total problem, not just the behavior.

Understand

Although it may be hard when both of you are in a conflict, try and understand your spouse. Put yourself in their shoes rather than focusing on who is winning or losing. This is not a sporting event. There are no winners or losers when it comes to marital conflict. No matter what the circumstances, being open and understanding can help ease the tension and resolve the problem much easier.

Listen carefully when your spouse comes to you with a problem. They may just be upset by something else and are just venting. The problem they present may seem trivial at the moment, but it means something to them, so taking the time to listen will help them calm down and see the problem for what it really is. Take some time to really try to understand what is going on in your spouse's mind. The better you can relate to your spouse, the better the solution that can be gained for the problem.

A great answer may not come right away. It may take some time on both parts to find a solution that will alleviate the circumstance to both of your satisfactions. Remember that you cannot just place a bandage over it and expect it to heal on its own. It's going to take some time and nurturing to get better!

Take action

Traditional approaches to mending a broken marriage may be ineffective because they emphasize listening instead of taking action. As a result, the couple concentrates on listening rather than doing. They can attend counseling sessions because the experience will give them a better understanding of their partner's point of view, but if no action is taken to fix the problem, further conflicts may wreck the marriage.

When you find a problem in your marriage, take time to discuss it, and then take time to think of reasonable solutions to the problem. Work together to implement those solutions so that the problem can be resolved rather that remaining a thorn in your side.

Troubled marriages change because of what people do. The changes happen because of what each spouse does, but you should always be patient with each other. You should take action instead of making promises and never following through. Remember, it's a two-sided deal. Your spouse needs to be just as willing as you are to take action and change the situation!

Leadership

A broken marriage needs some kind of leadership. After listening to each other, someone should have the courage to pave the way. This takes time and courage, but the results can change the entire course of the marriage. You may have a great understanding of your spouse's point of view, but it feels like it's just out there now, and there is nothing that is being done in order to resolve it.

Be the leader if nothing is happening. Implement the changes that are necessary in order to save your marriage. It won't be easy and there may be resistance from the other side, but the efforts will be respected once the conflicts are solved.

Don't try to be a hero. Just try to make the necessary changes happen in order to repair what is broken.

Conflicts are a normal part of every marriage. Some marriages will grow and thrive once they are resolved, while some problems will stagnate and cause even more conflict and tear a marriage apart. You're reading this book in order to save your marriage. It will not be an easy effort, but at least you've taken the first step to change. Be patient with your spouse. Talk to them. Encourage them. The better you are at resolving conflict will help you to heal what is broken much faster!

Chapter 3: How To Resolve Conflicts And Save Your Marriage

Your marriage may be at the brink of breaking down. Both of you may have had your share of disagreements and have lost trust and faith in each other. Instead of happiness, you have arguments, anger, hurtful feelings, disappointments, and frustrations. You can no longer go out as a couple like you used to without arguing, even in public places. You may be haunted by past hurts that were never resolved. Perhaps one, or both, of you could still be carrying baggage from your childhood that was never dealt with. You may also have disappointments stemming from unmet expectations.

When you got married, you might have had storybook expectations. You would have a picture perfect wedding, live in a clean and cheerful home, and have children. You would be happy. However, when your lives actually came together, you found that your expectations were not going to be met in the way that you wished for them to be. It may be that you and your spouse are simply set in your ways and need to learn how to make some changes. It could be that you don't want to change, but you want to change your spouse in order to meet your ideal. This is selfish and won't work if you wish to save a marriage.

Despite having a number of problems that cause conflicts, you can still resolve them and save your marriage. You can work as a couple, using the advice in this book, and put your marriage back together. However, this calls for hard work. Both of you need to be willing to do the work, otherwise you may fail to resolve the conflicts. If you cannot resolve them on your own, you may want to find a marriage counselor to help both of you.

First and foremost, you have to admit that there is conflict in your marriage. If one of you isn't sure that there is a problem, then they will not be in on trying to fix the problem. Be open with your communication. Tell your spouse what is bothering you. Let your spouse tell you what is bothering him or her. Having a strong start will help your chances at saving your marriage.

Resolving conflict requires you to know, accept, and adjust to each other

One reason why there are conflicts in many marriages is that couples don't understand, accept, or adjust to each other. Since opposites attract, you need to understand your spouse in detail. You might have thought that you knew your partner well, but when you started living under the same roof, you realized there was much you didn't know. Anything big or small triggers tension because you don't understand each other.

We discussed this in detail in the first chapter. Realizing that you are coming from two different lives and trying to make a new one is difficult. You both have your likes and dislikes, ways of doing things, and expectations for what your life together should look like. More than likely, these will all be different. You have to learn to live together and make changes that both of you can agree on. Understanding your partner is the first step in making the process easier.

You should take the time to learn about the other person's likes or dislikes. You also need to know how they behave in certain situations, their beliefs, values, interests, background, and expectations so you can accept and adjust to each other. No one is perfect and as much as you should not give excuses for bad habits and behavior, you should allow some room for differences. It is hard to change someone, so accepting your spouse and adjusting to each other is easier than trying to change them. It is important to have compromises when reaching an agreement becomes impossible. One has to understand where the other one is coming from in order to live in harmony.

Resolving conflict requires love-based confrontations

It is easier to resolve conflicts when both spouses love each other deeply. This occurs when each spouse feels that the other half is a good friend who listens, understands, and works through any conflicts. To do this requires love-based confrontations. Confronting your spouse with love requires humility, selflessness, patience, and wisdom. However, humility and selflessness doesn't mean being a doormat.

If you are at a point where you feel like the love is gone, you make the effort to confront your spouse in a loving manner. If your spouse feels like you're making an effort and that you do care, he or she will more likely to respond lovingly in return. However, how do you know that you're confronting your spouse in a loving manner?

Before confronting your spouse, check what your motivation is and whether it is right or wrong. Learn to approach your spouse lovingly. Before you act, ask yourself the following:

Will my words help or hurt my spouse?

If the confrontation is going to be a personal attack, then you know that you're not approaching the situation lovingly. When confronting your spouse, you want to help him or her grow along with your relationship.

When I bring this issue up, will it cause healing or isolation?

You need to learn to pick your battles. If the confrontation is necessary to heal your relationship, then it must happen. However, if you try to pick apart your spouse and his or her actions, then it will make the gap in your relationship even worse. Think about the outcome of your confrontation before addressing it with your partner.

Check your attitude and approach your spouse in a loving manner that portrays the following:

- I care about you
- I respect you
- I want the best for you
- I want you to respect me
- I am interested in knowing how you feel

You want to show your spouse that you care about resolving your differences. Instead of going forth selfishly, try going into the confrontation with your spouse's interests in mind. Being selfless will help resolve the situation much quicker than thinking about yourself and getting a quick fix to the problem.

Check the circumstances, which include:

Timing – avoid confronting your spouse when he or she is tired or busy. Putting another burden on your spouse's shoulders when he or she is not in the best mood can cause even more conflict. Find a time when you are both unoccupied and have time to listen to one another.

Location – avoid arguing before the children or in public. Your personal problems are just that: personal. Don't bring others into them. This will only make it seem like you're putting on a show to embarrass your partner. If the problem happens in a public place or in front of others, find a constructive time to approach the issue when it's just you and your spouse together.

Setup – you should never criticize, ridicule, or make fun of your spouse, especially in front of other people. You want the confrontation to be constructive. Don't make it seem like you're putting your spouse down. This will only amplify your current situation.

Consider other pressures that may be present. Become sensitive about your spouse and what is pressuring them. When tackling confrontations, be tactful and wise. Remember, you are two imperfect human beings trying to make your lives work together. Take that into account when you wish to work on your problems. You both carry the responsibility and burdens of saving your relationship.

Resolving conflict requires selflessness

Many differences are magnified because of selfishness. Everyone wants things their own way and no one wants to stoop low because this may be viewed as weakness. Fact is, a relationship should be about giving. You give up your interests and wants for your spouse. Your spouse should do the same for you.

Maintaining harmony in marriage has been difficult for many couples. When two people begin their marriage, and they try to go their own selfish ways, they can never experience the oneness of marriage. Many people are self-centered and they don't empathize or put themselves in their spouse's situation, which leads to conflicts. However, selflessness does not mean that you cannot pursue your dreams and goals, have a career, and be who you were meant to be. Your spouse should, in fact, encourage and support you so you can be happy and fulfilled.

Think about it as a union of interests. You support your spouse, and he or she in turn will support your goals and interests. Instead of focusing on yourself, focus on your spouse and let your spouse focus on you. Being selfless on both ends will help you grow and flourish as a couple, even when times are difficult.

You should be selfless. Find out what is the common good for both of you and your kids and empathize with one another. Have affection and compassion for each other and treat one another with humility. Marriage offers a great opportunity to do something for each other in a selfless way.

Resolving conflict requires you to pursue peace

You should live peacefully with your spouse. Many couples may find this hard. Living at peace means that you have to pursue peace. It means taking the initiative to resolve a conflict rather than waiting for your partner to take the first step. This may be difficult, especially if you are the one who has been offended, but, at times, it is the only way. For a long time I thought this was not right. I would wait for the other person to take a step, but it would never happen. Maybe he would never realize what he had done or he didn't know what to do. Finally, I decided to take the initiative to resolve the conflict, even though I was the one who was hurting and the other person was relieved. I have done this ever since. My spouse never even realized that he had hurt me until I brought it up. You cannot expect your spouse to be a mind-reader. Sometimes, you have to be the one to put your hurts in the open and ask for help in healing them.

Pursuing peace and finding a resolution to the conflict means setting aside your own hurtful feelings, anger, and bitterness to find a solution. Apply this in all other areas of your life, with your children, parents, family members, colleagues, and friends. If you don't feel at peace with yourself and your own circumstances, then your entire world will feel jumbled and chaotic.

Resolving conflicts means to "fight fair"
There is nothing worse than arguments that go nowhere. Many times they leave you feeling even more hurt than before. These arguments are the ones that are aimed at hurting your spouse rather than trying to find a solution to the problem. This is never a good circumstance because someone is bound to come out of the confrontation hurting.

During any discussion, try to handle only one issue at a time and mainly the most recent. When you bring up several issues at the same time and you dig up past hurts, you get further away from solving the problem. Avoid accumulating a load of complaints to deal with at once. Resolve one issue at a time.

There is a saying "forgive and forget." Forgetting may not be easy, but forgiving requires that you put the past to rest. Let the past remain in the past. If you have forgiven a situation before, don't try to dig it back up to make your present argument stronger. It will only hurt both you and your spouse in the end.

Resolving conflict requires forgiveness
Forgiveness is a two-way street, but even when the other person fails to forgive, do your part. There is no relationship that can blossom without forgiveness because no matter how hard you try to love each other, you will fail at one time or another. Failure causes hurtful feelings and the only way to resolve this is to forgive.

To maintain a happy marriage, you need to ask for forgiveness and grant it quickly before conflicts breed resentment, which leads to bitterness. When you eagerly ask for forgiveness, you pursue oneness rather than isolation. The ultimate relief for any hurt is forgiveness. The other person may not always ask for forgiveness, but when you forgive, you set yourself free.

Since conflict is going to arise in any marriage, learning to resolve it quickly and peacefully is crucial to being able to move on. You and your spouse may not have such a good track record when it comes to this. You may have many problems that tend to recycle themselves, creating one huge problem. Find a place to start. Agree to disagree. Learn to respect your spouse and make it about them rather than about you.

The better you handle a conflict, the easier it is to resolve it and move forward. Start small and work on your problems one at a time. This is a process that can take some time, but if both you and your spouse are invested in the process, you will both come out winners in the end.

Chapter 4: Restoring Love In Your Marriage

At one time, Sue really loved her husband, Bill. However, as time went by, she let the little things about him bother her. After a while, she even came to resent him. One day, she sat down and thought about what had gone wrong in their marriage. Why had the love slipped away? How could she find ways to restore it? Sue knew that she had to let some things go, but she had no idea where to begin. She knew that they started their marriage on a strong and loving foundation, and she wanted to get their relationship back to where it was before it seemed to fall to pieces.

Love is the strong foundation upon which marriage is based. Typically, people get married because of the love they have for each other. If everything else fails, the couple should restore their love because it is what makes them stay together. Love is the glue that holds them together as one. When love feels like it's failing, then your foundation is going to crumble. How do you repair a crumbling foundation? You can work on restoring the love that brought you and your spouse together.

Restoring love

You should know that there is no such thing as a perfect marriage. A marriage may look free of conflicts, but that is an illusion. This is due to the fact that each individual has his or her own inborn characteristic traits and personality, different experiences, backgrounds, beliefs, values, and interests from the other. Every couple is made up of two very distinct, different people. They have had different experiences and, as a result, different emotional make-ups. Couples can create some compatibility within the marriage, but a husband and wife will always have different perspectives about issues, which can create conflict. There are conflicts about handling money, careers, the in-laws, rearing the children, and many other issues that are common in any marriage. This can be complicated further by the loss of a job, unemployment, sickness in the family, loss of a home, and extra-marital affairs, among other things married people go through.

One spouse may be a spendthrift while the other one likes accounting for every coin. One parent can be a disciplinarian while the other one may disagree with the treatment the kids are given. One parent may be authoritative while the other may be permissive. Whatever the differences may be, it may cause conflicts if not handled the right way. You may want to live in the city while your spouse longs for life in rural areas.

In order to make any marriage work, you will have to compromise and listen to your spouse. Knowing that both of you come from diverse backgrounds, you will want to find a common ground on how to handle circumstances in your life. If you haven't done so before, think of some "what if" scenarios and get an idea of how you or your spouse would handle it if it should come to be. This will give you a good idea of both of your viewpoints on certain circumstances so that they don't come as a total surprise if the event should come to pass.

There are couples who feel that if they could get rid of conflicts they could be happy, but there are still couples who live happily in spite of the conflicts. Happiness is relative. There can be happiness even when some conflicts are not fully resolved. The difference between a couple that lives happily and one that regrets ever having met and married each other is love. You can never be free of conflict, but if you love each other, you will find ways to resolve your differences. Whether you have happiness in your marriage or not depends on whether you are in love with each other. Love is the glue that will bind you together, even when times get tough. Knowing that you love your spouse and that love is returned to you, you will be more willing to work out the conflicts in a civil and loving manner.

Restoring and sustaining love in a marriage is more important than resolving conflicts. If you restore your love for one another, you will easily resolve conflicts because you care for each other. For those conflicts that are not solvable, you will need to agree to disagree and move on. If you don't like a particular thing, you don't have to. We can respect each other's differences and move on. I don't have to be you and you don't have to be me, but as long as we love and respect each other, we can complement each other and embrace our differences. Finding a middle ground is much nicer than being in constant conflict with your spouse.

To love each other and resolve conflicts are both important factors in a marriage, but love takes the top priority. You should resolve your conflicts by using steps and strategies that build your love.

How to build your love

Most marriage counselors are focused on conflict resolution because that is what couples tell them they want. However, building your love for each other should be the first priority. Many couples seek help to resolve their conflicts, not to restore their feelings of love. Couples should see the importance of being in love because many problems arise from loss of love. This is the real issue in many marriages, but there are couples who believe that love cannot be restored to the level it once was.

Couples assume their marriage will survive if they are able to resolve their conflicts and have their own lifestyles. They think that it is normal to lose passion in a marriage, and they can still remain together. However, happily married couples do more than resolve their conflicts. They work hard to preserve their feelings of love for each other. Many couples who resolve conflicts still divorce. That is why restoring love is so important to saving your marriage.

What made you love your spouse in the beginning? How can you find those feelings of love once more? Knowing why you love your spouse and the qualities that you love about him or her will help you to rebuild love when it seems to have totally disappeared. Think of the things that made you fall in love. Knowing specific reasons why you love your spouse will make it easier to resolve conflicts in your marriage.

Create a plan to restore your love

Think of marriage as a love bank account where you can deposit and withdraw love. Your love for each other can be deposited and withdrawn from the love account. Almost everything you and your spouse do either deposits or withdraws love. Since most of what you do becomes a habit, you should deposit love continually instead of withdrawing it. Such habits play an important role in creating or destroying your love for each other.

Your love can last for a lifetime if you avoid withdrawing love unnecessarily and keep depositing more love.

The following steps will help you:

- Make a commitment to create and sustain love in your marriage
- Identify habits that destroy love and avoid them
- Build love and overcome conflicts in a loving manner
- Identify the most important emotional needs of your spouse and learn to meet those needs

Having a plan to build the balance of your account rather than drain it will help you from going bankrupt in the love department. No marriage can survive if there isn't love to fund it. Make it a habit to show your spouse that you love him or her on a daily basis. Feed your love rather than take from it.

Have an effective conflict resolution plan

If you do not have an effective plan of action to resolve conflicts and save your marriage, it is unlikely that you will achieve the marriage objectives you have set. For many couples, marriage is an area where effective planning of objectives is often disregarded or considered unnecessary. Many couples assume their instincts will guide them whenever they have conflicts.

We have all been in a confrontation. Our brains tend to focus on how we can survive the fight and come out unscathed. This usually triggers our flight or fight instinct. When the fight becomes imminent, we will do whatever we can to come out on top. This is unhealthy because we are focusing on self-preservation rather than constructive resolution.

Couples should have plans instead of relying on their instincts. Many times people revert to anger, disrespect, arguments, demands, and blame while trying to resolve their conflicts. This will only end in worse problems in the end.

As for emotional needs in marriage, there are spouses who believe that they should do what they feel like doing. The idea of creating plans to meet your spouse's emotional needs, whether you feel like doing it or not, is not embraced by many spouses even though it should. Applying emotional intelligence is vital in your marriage. This means knowing how to deal with yours and other people's emotions. Remember, you took on a commitment to take care of your spouse, so being emotionally selfish will only tear the relationship apart.

Having a plan in place for you to resolve conflicts is very crucial in handling conflicts when they arise. Instead of creating and implementing a plan to resolve marital conflicts, some couples revert to demands, arguments, disrespect, and anger. These instincts destroy their love for each other and fail to provide the couple with long-term solutions. When couples don't know any better, they keep repeating those mistakes until their love turns to hate.

You need to create a well-conceived plan you will implement when resolving your conflicts so you can restore and sustain your love for each other. This way, your marriage will be successful and you will be happy because conflicts will not jeopardize your love.

What are some elements that can make your plan effective? When my spouse and I get into an argument, I find it helpful to walk away for five or ten minutes until I can calm my emotions and think rationally about what is happening. We have come to an understanding that I need that time in order to regain my rational thinking because I tend to lash out to keep myself from losing the argument.

Think of what could help you to achieve a peaceful resolution to your problem in a loving way. If you are hot-headed, maybe you need to take five or ten minutes to get your thoughts in order so that you don't end up making the argument worse than what it started out to be.

Elements of a loving conflict resolution plan include:

- Listening to your spouse
- Having your spouse listen to you
- Talk about the differences in opinion
- Find a common ground
- Respect the decision on both ends

Building love in conflict may be tough, but your relationship will grow even stronger because of it. You are team working together, so make sure that team is built on a solid and loving foundation.

Chapter 5: Choosing A Marriage Counselor

You need help, now! Your marriage is quickly falling apart, and you cannot have a civil conversation. There needs to be a mediator. That is where a marriage counselor can help open up the lines of communication. However, the list of marriage counselors is as long as there are minutes in the day. How do you choose one that is right for you?

Therapists come in many different types and styles. You should, therefore, ask yourself the following questions:

- What should I look for in a marriage counselor?
- What kind of therapist is right for both of us?

When my spouse and I were having problems in our marriage, the only thing that we could think of was to have a marriage counselor help us through the rut. We weren't communicating in a healthy manner, and that only caused recurring problems. When we decided to make this move, it overwhelmed us. What therapist would be right for our situation? In the end, we went to our church and asked for a referral. We wanted to talk to someone who shared our belief system, which included lifelong marriage. The first counselor seemed to not be a good match for us. We felt like we were getting nowhere with him. Finally, we found a great counselor who focused on our needs for love and conflict resolution.

Although different marriage counselors have their own strategies which they emphasize, those who focus on restoring love and conflict resolution have the highest levels of success. You can ask for referrals from family and friends. Search for marriage counselors who are trustworthy and respected. If either of you doesn't feel comfortable with a therapist, choose another one. Look for someone you can strike a rapport with.

Couples should look for a marriage counselor who can help them restore their love, restructure their communication, and show them how to deal with the real situation, not digging the past. Couples might be encouraged to explore the impact that their past has on their marriage, but only to the extent for this to help.

Dwelling too much on the past may create more problems instead of resolving the issue. The goal should be to rebuild love that has been lost and resolve important issues to help the couple stay together. When one spouse gets angry, the ideal strategy is for the other to soothe him or her. This will strengthen their relationship and help save the marriage. In some cases, this is not the natural instinct of one or both parties involved in the marriage. This may be a learned behavior.

Couples also benefit greatly from fair fighting, whereby each partner is given the chance to talk while the other one listens without interruptions. When couples talk to each other on their own, they may become defensive or strike back with hurtful insults. They also dig deep into the past. Fair fighting means learning to hear the other one through, without the interruptions that only escalate the conflict.

What should we look for in a therapist?

Neutral
Sometimes one spouse will come to feel the therapist has colluded with their partner against them. In such instances, the aggrieved spouse may not feel the need to share and may become withdrawn. If your spouse feels this way, perhaps it would be best to seek help from another counselor, one who can strike a better sense of neutrality as the sessions go on.

Common beliefs
We all hold different values and beliefs. For example, you don't want to go to a Christian marriage counselor if you're an atheist. The counselor doesn't share your worldview, and that will make it difficult to get what you need from him or her. Take some time and find someone who shares your core beliefs and values. Maybe make a list of two or three to try out and see if they are able to help.

Focused on building love

If the counselor's sole focus is on conflict resolution, a huge piece of your marriage puzzle is not being put together. Sure, couples do need to learn how to resolve conflicts, but that alone will not lend itself to a successful marriage. Learning how to build love through your conflict resolution will help you to come together on more than one level, making your marriage even stronger than it was to begin with.

Helps find solutions

You want a counselor who will help you to solve your problems. They can do so by giving you exercises or suggestions on handling certain situations. One of the best pieces of advice our counselor gave us was to have a time frame set aside on a daily basis where we could discuss our day and bring up any concerns to be discussed. We found that our conflict arose from the fact that we spent so much time apart that we had trouble spending time together,

A marriage counsel is not the ultimate answer to all of your marital problems. That gives them way too much responsibility over your life. Know that they are there as a mediator to help you strengthen what has been weakened due to conflict and time. If you wish to rescue your marriage based upon visiting a marriage counselor, your intentions are ill-placed. You and your spouse have to be the ones to do the work. The counselor is just a mediator who can help you get back on the right track.

Once you find a marriage counselor who you feel comfortable with and will help you resolve your problems, give therapy a chance. Believe that your marriage can be rescued from what many others have. However, be ready to do what it takes and work to save your marriage. Therapy is not easy, but if you and your spouse truly love each other, you will save your marriage, forever.

Commit to visiting your counselor on a regular basis. After a while, you will find that you need to spend less time in the office and you can resolve your conflicts on your own. The counselor is great to have for a season. You may even find that you will have more than one season that needs the help of a counselor. That's okay. You're showing yourself and your spouse that you care enough about your relationship to seek help.

Chapter 6: Turning Conflict Into Ways To Grow

Take a moment and think about the first time you met your spouse. What struck you about him or her? Was it their mannerisms, the way they looked? Look at your spouse now. What still strikes you about him or her? Is it different than when you first met?

As you get to know your spouse, you both grow and learn more about one another. Your initial response to them may be a thing of the past. After a few conversations with them, you may find that you enjoy their personality and sense of humor much more than the way they smile.

Conflicts are a normal part of any relationship. Some conflicts can be good. You learn that something that you once thought was fine really isn't after all. By learning where you are wrong and taking responsibility for your wrongs, you are growing as a person. You may not know what you're doing wrong until you have an unavoidable conflict.

Knowing what you love about your spouse will help you to keep focused on the end result of the conflicts that will arise during your time together. If all you focus on is the problems of your marriage, then you will lack the ambition to save your marriage for the right reasons. Resolving a conflict in a civil manner is nice, but it's also nice to know that the person on the other end of the conflict still loves you for who you are and what you stand for. That is a valuable feeling to carry with you.

As a couple, you want to learn to grow together. This cannot be done without learning about one another and having some conflict along the way. Think of conflict as growing pains. In order to reach an end result, you want to get past the worst of the problems and look forward to the bright future ahead. Taking the time to figure out what is bothering your spouse and how you can fix it in order to make him or her happier is just one way to show your love for each other.

Using your conflict as a way to grow is not only a constructive way to view it, but it will also help you to resolve it in a more loving and gentle manner. When the focus is off of you and your desires, then the conflicts are resolved in a nicer and much more amiable manner. We are all human and we are not perfect. Mistakes are going to be made, so why not use these mistakes to make you a better person and improve your relationship with your spouse?

Look at conflict as a chance to learn

We all make mistakes. People will learn from mistakes. Think of conflict in the same way. Something brought you and your spouse to the point where something must be resolved. A mistake needs to be rectified. Taking the time to work through the problem and coming to a conclusion together will help you to both grow and learn.

Don't go into it as being defensive. This is the worst attitude to have. First of all, it's selfish. You are out to protect yourself, no matter what the cost. Secondly, you will not be open to seeing your spouse's point of view, which totally defeats the purpose of confrontation. Go into the conversation with an open mind and an understanding mindset. This will help both of you to resolve your differences without the situation turning into a full on fight.

If you approach conflict as a way to learn more about yourself and your spouse, then you will find that conflict resolution can take place in a more loving and constructive way. You may have to make the same mistake a few times to learn from it, but once it's engrained in your mind, it will be a memory!

Learn from your past mistakes

Many of us will repeat a past mistake over and over again. It's not that we don't feel bad about what we have done. It's because we are human and we tend to make mistakes. When you find that a certain method of conflict resolution hasn't worked out in the past, then stop trying to use it. Learn from your past mistakes and move on to your future!

Knowing that you have a conflict to face and resolve can be stress provoking. However, finding a solution to the problem and learning from the situation will help you grow as a person and learn to avoid such mistakes in the future. You may not even realize that you have made a mistake until your spouse comes to you hurt and angry.

Not only should you learn from your past actions, you should also learn from the ways in which you handled the situations in the past. Knowing that lashing back at your spouse in anger is not the best method of conflict resolution will help you to avoid using it when the next conflict comes along. This will help you both hone in on the best way to solve your problems. Since every couple is different, what works for your conflict resolution may not work in another marriage.

Put your spouse's feelings before your own

Many of us can be selfish by nature. It has been taught to us to be that way. You have probably heard people talking about looking out for number one. In marriage, you're not the number one. You should save that spot for your spouse. Think about how he or she would feel in the situation. When you put their feelings before yours, then you won't be as defensive and out to get your way. This will help the solution be more amicable for both of you.

Your spouse should carry the same viewpoint on conflict. A loving marriage requires that you put your spouse before yourself. Put yourself in his or her shoes before you even bring up the situation. If you cannot do this, then step away from the conflict until you can do this. Your emotions may stop you from putting your spouse's thoughts and feelings before your own, so talk about them when you are both calm and rational.

Growing in your marriage should be the first priority. Just getting by isn't good for either one of you. Learn from one another and learn from your past conflicts. Use the past to help you heal the present. Don't dwell on the past, but focus on the future. No matter what, we are all students in life, and marriage is no exception to this rule! Learn from your mistakes and use them to build a strong and healthy relationship!

Chapter 7: Tips For Starting A Productive Conversation

Since you are seeking some advice on how to rescue your marriage by handling conflicts better, it is essential that you approach a conflict and a conversation in a productive and caring manner. In past chapters, I have mentioned that it is extremely important not to speak in anger. Anger is one way to make your situation much worse than it already is. You also don't want to go into a conversation acting like the issue is not a big deal. If it's affecting your marriage, it's a big deal!

In this chapter, I am going to provide some suggestions on how to start a productive conversation that will yield desirable results. Some of us just don't know how to go about starting a conversation, especially if the topic is heavy and we are worried about the potential outcome. Just remember, your spouse may be just as nervous about starting the conversation as you are!

Before you begin

If something is bothering you, you don't want to let the problem go on for a long period of time. You want to have some resolution to the problem so that you can grow from it and put it behind you. However, the problem may be something that is making you incredibly angry or emotional. How do you begin a conversation if you have so many negative emotions going on?

Take some time to calm yourself down before you delve into the conversation. If you start it out by being worked up, then you are going to put those emotions into the conversation, and you might not get the results from the confrontation that you were hoping for.

Take ten minutes to cool your emotions

Since your emotional state can affect the course of a conversation, if you feel anger or any other strong emotion that may get in the way of having a complete conversation, take some time to let those emotions cool before heading into the topic. If you encounter an argument and you're already angry and ready to fight, the outcome will not be as desired. If your spouse confronts you with a problem and you're feeling

41

negative emotions, don't be afraid to ask for a few minutes to cool down before discussing the topic. This will make for a more civil conversation which will see positive results.

Don't pursue the issue until you can see the other person's point of view

If you're trying to lick your own wounds to begin with, you will not be able to see your spouse's side of the argument. You probably won't even try to. You will go in kicking to begin with. In cases like this, take some time to focus on how your spouse may be feeling. Once you can get a sense of the other side, then you can enter into a civil conversation where you're not out to win a fight.

Gauge your spouse's emotional state before bringing up the topic

Just like you don't want to go into a conversation when you're feeling anger and resentment, don't try to bring up one with your spouse when they are in the same state of mind. Try to get a feel for your spouse's mood before bringing up a topic. If they are already in a negative mood, the conversation will not end well. You are just looking for a fight.

Beginning a healthy conversation starts even before the subject is brought up. If a marriage is in trouble, many of the conversations may already be negative. You may be ready to fight already. However, fighting, being defensive and blaming your spouse will not help find a reasonable solution to the problem. Take some time to think about how you want the conversation to progress before going into it. If it does turn negative, then be prepared to keep yourself from lashing out.

How to approach the subject

Once you feel like you can enter a conversation and make some progress on the conflict, it's time to set forth and approach your spouse. Sometimes, your spouse may not even know that there was a problem, so this might be a complete shock to them. Be as gentle as possible. Here are a few ways to ease into the conversation without making it seem like you're attacking.

Approach your partner gently

The approach to a conversation can make a world of difference in the way in which it will progress. If you go into the conversation already sure that you're right and your spouse is wrong, it isn't going to end well. Remember, you are both human and see things differently. Your spouse may think that they are right from the beginning and that will result in a battle with no positive outcome. Take a moment and think about how to bring up the subject. Be gentle. Try using gentle phrases rather than commands. Try:

- "Can we talk?" rather than "we need to talk."
- "May I have a moment?" rather than "I need to talk to you about something."
- "When you have a moment," rather than "This needs to happen right now."

Be compassionate instead of commanding. Yes, the conversation needs to take place, but using strong commands to begin with will only set a negative tone to the conversation. You want open and honest communication, not a fight.

Use words to describe your feelings, not accusing words towards your spouse

One of the main mistakes that couples make in conflict resolution is to place blame on the other party. When this happens, it takes any sort of responsibility off of you. A problem is a two-sided ordeal, not just placing blame and moving on. This not only breaks your spouse's spirit, but it will also take away from their self-confidence and their ability to please you as their spouse.

When approaching the subject, even if you feel like your spouse is wrong, do not openly use words that accuse them. Try focusing on your feelings rather than their actions.

43

- "I feel bad because of what happened."
- "When this happened, it made me feel…"
- "When you said that, it made me feel…"

By putting your feelings first, you are not attacking your partner by making them feel guilty. Coming across as being accusing in the beginning will only shut down the lines of communication before you have a chance to get started.

Try to understand your spouse's thoughts and reactions

Carrying on a good and productive conversation takes two parties. In order for that to happen, you have to be empathetic. Try to understand your spouse's thoughts and feelings. The more you can see the other point of view, the less likely you will be to place blame and accuse your spouse of wrongdoing. You never know, you may have been wrong to begin with!

Starting a difficult conversation can be tough, especially if you and your spouse are already on rocky terms. However, the lines of communication need to be opened up in order for you to forgive and move on. If you hold on to hard feelings and resentment, it will only make it more difficult to work things out with your spouse. Since starting the conversation itself can be difficult, make it as smooth of a start as you possibly can.

Handling hurtful accusations and comments

Words can hurt. And when we are angry and ready to fight, those words will come bursting forth without much thought behind them. Sadly, these are the most damaging words that can be said. If you could take some of the words you have spoken in the past back, would you? Almost everyone I know would adamantly say "Yes!" So, when you go into a conversation and your spouse is already fired up and ready to fight, it's important that you try to handle some of these words lightly. They are spoken in anger, making them much worse than they should be.

On the flip side, you don't want to feed into that anger by launching a counterattack. That will do nothing to resolve the conflict. Learning to handle harsh words and accusations during a confrontation can show your spouse love and understanding. Let's take a look at a few tips on how you can handle these outbursts without making any outbursts of your own.

Don't reply in a like manner if your spouse is angry

It may seem like the easiest way to respond. Your spouse is yelling and saying negative things to and about you. You want to do the same. Make him or her feel the way that they are making you feel at this very moment. However, if you stop to think about it, how productive is that? Think about the outcome of your reaction. If they are too emotional to handle a civil conversation, you may need to stop right there and come back when they have had time to cool down. Don't fuel their fire by responding with accusations and insults. They hurt both of you.

Stay calm even if your spouse is not

Depending on the situation, you may not see it as being as big of a deal as your spouse may. This can result in strong reactions whenever the topic is brought up. However, you know that the problem needs to be resolved somehow. Even if your spouse starts out by being angry and fueled up, the best thing that you can do is to stay calm and not fight back. The situation can escalate out of control quickly if both of you are not calm and rational. If it comes down to it, tell your spouse that you can continue the conversation when he or she has had time to calm down a little. This might aggravate them, but in the end, it will stop the problem from escalating even more than it already has.

Try to encourage your spouse to calm down, even if it means postponing the conversation

Since every person is different, this may or may not work in your situation. Personally, I get angrier when I'm told to calm down. For some, your spouse may see the reason behind calming down and it can help the situation get better. When I'm fired up, it takes some time for me to cool down. My spouse has learned to understand this and makes certain that the conversation happens when I can think more clearly. This may take some time to happen, but it's incredibly important that both parties are calm and rational in order to get the best results from the conversation.

Having a calm and collected conversation will help you to solve your issues better than if you are going at them filled with emotion. Remember that. This not only will show you and your spouse that you can solve problems adequately, but it also shows that you care enough about one another to take the time to prepare for a civil conversation. As mentioned before, marriage rescue should be placed upon love, and that will make resolving conflict easier and more fruit-bearing.

Empathize rather than get defensive

Learning to empathize with your spouse, even if you don't agree, is a great way to help the conflict resolution process. By taking the time to try and see their side of the story, you are showing caring and compassion for their thoughts and feelings, rather than being focused on your own. This might be a difficult thing to do at first, but the more that you get to know your spouse and how he or she reacts to certain circumstances, this can get easier and your arguments can be settled in a loving manner.

Stay true to your viewpoint without getting angry

When fighting, it might be easier to give in to the other person's point of view simply to make peace. This isn't the best way to resolve a problem. This will only cause it to become a recurring problem because you still hold to your own viewpoint even though you gave in to stop the argument. This may happen if your spouse has a more commanding personality than yours. You may feel more at peace by giving in because it stops the confrontation. However, this can be hurtful to you later on. When discussing a problem, hold true to your viewpoint. Unless your spouse can provide compelling evidence to change your mind, don't give in unless you know that the other point of view really is what you agree with.

Control your initial thoughts and feelings when getting defensive
It may seem natural to fire back an insult when one is given. This is not productive to your situation. In order to stop yourself from firing insults back, you need to learn to control your thoughts and feelings when the unexpected happens. As much as you would like to think that you can control what will happen in the confrontation, you know that that will not happen. By learning to control your thoughts and anger before they can come out in the midst of an argument, you are not letting your spouse get under your skin the way that they are trying to. Some people feed off of confrontation, but that will not achieve a desirable outcome.

Understand that your spouse may be on the defensive
Before you get angry, it may be essential that you identify that your spouse is already on the defense. This will only make the situation more difficult to talk about. When this is the case, you need to approach carefully, using words and phrases that will take down the defensive attitude. It is also important not to attack when trying to get your spouse to the point where you are not arguing, but you are discussing.

Empathy can go a long way. Remember this when you know that there is a problem in your marriage the needs to be addressed. You are not at battle with one another. You are trying to understand one another so that you can put your differences behind you and move on. Try approaching your problems with empathy rather than anger. See how much further you can go with it!

Allow your spouse to speak their mind
In every marriage, there is always the one spouse who is more verbal and commanding than the other. This is the person who often controls the conversation. When you have conflicts, this is not a good thing. This is putting the dominant spouse in control of the situation, making it impossible for both parties to be satisfied with the conclusion of the

problem. In a good, conflict-resolving conversation, it is important that you are both heard, no matter which one of you is the more dominant of the two!

Don't dominate the situation

If you are the spouse who tends to dominate, STOP! You need to let your spouse have a voice and express their thoughts. This might be a difficult thing to give up at first. However, once you start to realize that your spouse has a mind of his or her own, it will be easier to turn the floor over to them. When you feel like you need to take control, take a step back and close your mouth. Let them speak. Listen. This will get far better results than you dictating the situation.

Allow for complete communication

Complete communication includes both sides. In the past, it may have seemed like one person made all of the decisions, including how a conversation went. This won't help you have long and lasting relationship. A relationship takes two, and two people need to be a part of the conversation. You had your say? Great, now let your spouse have theirs!

Communication is a huge part of rescuing a marriage. Even though love has a great role in making it heal, you have to be able to talk through your conflicts and find reasonable solutions to your problems. In the past, you may have found that this has been difficult. You or your spouse may rely on emotions when resolving conflict. One spouse may be more dominant than the other. However, by getting to know these characteristics in each other, you will find a way to have a conversation that will be beneficial for both parties.

Remember, love is the key to a lasting marriage. Find that love and let the conflicts be resolved through love and understanding. Even though the lines of communication may be down right now, work on building a healthy and happy marriage by opening up communication and allowing each other to be mutual parties in conflict resolution!

Conclusion

Thank you again for purchasing this book!

I sincerely hope that it was able to help you to see the steps and strategies you should take to rescue your marriage. Keep in mind that all marriages go through trials and tribulations. It seems as though couples focus on the things they have in common when they are first dating, and even within the first few months or even years of their marriage. However, inevitably, there comes a time in every marriage when the couple starts to focus more on the things that they don't have in common. That's usually when the issues begin to arise.

This is why it is so important to always think back at what brought you both together. Make it a habit to regularly talk about past dates, trips, jokes, movies, dinners, etc. Then take it one step further relive some of those moments. In doing so, you will keep the love alive in your marriage. As I always say, when there is love, everything else will just fall into place.

Before you go, could you please do me a favor? If you enjoyed this book, would you be kind enough as to leave a positive review on Amazon? Your review would help me to build up the credibility of this book and allow for it to reach and help more individuals as I hope that it has helped you.

Also, if you would like to be notified whenever I publish a new book, or to access my FREE book promotions, just click on this link RoldanBooks.com/AlexisOptin to join my email list.

Thank you and good luck!

Made in the USA
Middletown, DE
27 March 2016